Welcome to the Navigate Bible study series. This Bible study series is specifically designed to be taught to young adults between the ages of 18 and 35. During this critical period, young people make life-time decisions in their career, family, spiritual life, and finances. It is our prayer that this Bible study series will be used to help young adults across the world that are on their life journey to navigate their course by using the principles given to us in the Bible.

This Bible study series is uniquely designed to be practical and applicable for use in any setting, such as Sunday School classes, cell groups, home Bible study groups, campus ministry meetings, individual devotion time, and countless other possibilities.

We are excited to announce that we have revamped our format. More discussion has been added because sometimes young people need to hear from each other as well as the teacher. These lessons are formerly published in the former Navigate Bible study series, and reformatted into our new user-friendly Navig8 format. Each lesson contains:

- *A Synopsis* to give you a general idea of the lesson and topic
- *An Introduction* to get your group to engage in thinking about your main topic including some Ice-Breakers.
- *Eight thought-provoking Bible-based questions* to explorer and discuss the topic effectively
- *A Conclusion* that gets your group to act upon principles that we have examined

It is our prayer that you will use Navig8 to challenge this generation of young adults to not only know the Word but live the Word through actively thinking through these powerful Bible principles. If you have any comments, please feel free to let us know.

In His service,

Hiro Nishi
Texas Hyphen // College & Career Director <txhyphen.com>

This Bible study series is sponsored and coordinated by Hyphen: College & Career Young Adults a ministry of the Texas District United Pentecostal Church – Youth Department.

A special thank you to our talented editor, Brother Drew Lynch. I appreciate the sacrifice of his time and gift for this project. I am grateful to know this talented and passionate man. Thank you also to Rev. Darrell McCoy for lending Bro. Lynch to us. I would also like to thank the Texas District board and Youth Department for allowing us to do this project. My mentors and pastors have influenced this project in many ways and I am grateful for them: L. Charles Treadway, D G Hargrove, and the late Allan Oggs, Sr.

Synopsis:

Developing and maintaining our relationships is important. None as important as our relationship with the one looking back through the mirror! Our self-image is an important aspect of our self. How we see ourselves and how God sees us can sometimes differ. We should strive to align ours vision with Gods!

Ice-Breaker:

- **Did Adam have a belly button?**
- **Would any of you feel comfortable vandalizing or speaking negatively about your church?**

Introduction:

Our Self-Image will influence every other relationship we have in life. Our relationship with others, our relationship with God, our actions and our attitudes will all be influenced by how we look at ourselves. A poor self-image can keep us from reaching our full potential. As we are charting the course of relationships in our lives, it's first important for us to look at the relationship with ourselves. Let's explore this topic further.

Question One: Who or what defines you as a person and in what ways?

- Your relationships
- Your past
- Jesus!

Question Two:Read **Genesis 1:27**. What does it mean to be made in God's image?

- We physically bear resemblance to God
- We have some of the same attributes and characteristics of God
- We are unique and different, like He is

Question Three: What are some ways to perpetuate a negative self-image?

- Continuously hold on to our past mistakes, beat ourselves up
- Listen to what the world and the enemy has to say about us, believing the lies they tell or false standards they set (i.e. beauty, clothing styles etc)
- Lack of worship or prayer, loss of how God sees us

Question Four: So how exactly does God see us? Read I Peter 2:9.What does this verse tell us about God's view of us?

- God sees us in a very positive light, as His royal, peculiar and priestly people
- God has chosen us! Remember, many are called but few are chosen! We are special if He has chosen us.
- God trusts us to accomplish something, to shew forth His praises to the world!

Question Five: How can our negative self-image harm others?

- A negative self-image can produce a poor attitude and bring others down

- Our lifestyle and actions can project on to others and harm them

- If we don't feel like we have anything to share with others, we won't and our witness will be silenced and souls may be lost because of it!

Question Six: Read **I Corin. 3:16**. How does realizing that we are God's temple affect our self-image?

- Positive impact! Even if we have many faults and weaknesses, if God now dwells in us our self-image should skyrocket!

- Give us a drive to do better and improve, knowing that we are God's temple should make us want to be the absolute best we can be

- It can also humble us, to realize that the Holiest of Holies now lives inside of us, we should be more careful of what we do or say.

Question Seven: Read **Proverbs 23:7**. What does this scripture mean to you and how does it apply to our discussion?

- We have tremendous power in determining who we are
- Thinking positive will produce positive and vice versa
- Our heart is the real issue, our heart needs to be right with God and then we will see us how He does

Question Eight: What are some steps to getting/maintaining a positive self image?

- Pray and ask God's help, get our heart and spirit right with God

- Work on the things that can be changed to improve ourselves and let God deal with the things we cannot.

- Surround yourself with Godly friends who are positive and can help uplift you and/or remind you just how awesome you are!

Conclusion:

Before we can ever have a positive, lasting, relationship with someone else we must first have a positive relationship with our self! We must realize that God has made us in His image. He knew us before we were made and knew exactly what we would be like, our weaknesses and strengths, failures and victories and yet He loved us. We must learn to see ourselves as God sees us, as His children, the people who are called by His name, the people that He shed his Blood for, the people He has filled with His Spirit, His home! Even if we have things that need to change, God wants to help us do it. We shouldn't let anything come between how God thinks about and sees us and how that affects our lives and the lives of everyone else we come into contact with. Maintaining a healthy, positive self-image is a must for proper relationship with God, and therefore a must for proper relationships with other people, especially those whom we hope to win! Spend some time in prayer and ask God to help you become the person He planned for.

Synopsis:

Our relationshipwith God is the single most important relationship a human being is fortunate enough to have. God is our source of everything, without Him we have nothing, are nothing and will be nothing. With Him however, we have everything we need or could ever dream of or desire. Where is our relationship at?

Ice-Breaker:

- **Anyone ever been totally without power? How long? How did it feel?**
- **What do you think God looks like? Young? Old? Middle-Eastern?**

Introduction:

Imagine a great power outage! Imagine the darkness and total absence of light and power. How gloomy and bleak is the picture? Now imagine you have this awesome lamp and it not only gives off light but also the power for other things as well. How awesome the lamp is! How bright, how powerful and useful! Totally different picture right? Problem is - the lamp must be plugged in to the source of power! So to must you and I! God is our source, we must be plugged in to Him! Our relationship with God is the most important relationship and must be cultivated, cared for and sought after above anything else!

Question One: Think for a moment: God is the source of???

- Strength
- Joy
- Peace
- Power
- Blessing
- Wisdom
- Knowledge
- Patience
- Fruits of the Spirit – Galatians 5:22-23

Question Two: Read Hebrews 11. What did the "heroes" of faith do to establish their relationship?

- Abel: Offered sacrifice
- Enoch: Diligently sought after God
- Noah: Worked
- Abraham: Obeyed
- Isaac: Blessed others
- Moses: Led others to God's promise
- Rahab: Risked

Question Three: What was the common denominator for all of their relationship with God?

- Faith >> The foundation of the relationship with God must be faith, and the faith leads us into the relationship with God.

Question Four: Is faith alone enough? Why or Why not?

- Lead them to read James 2:14 and 26 According to James, you must have works or actions to follow the faith. As we fill ourselves with faith, we must also learn to fill ourselves with fruits or works. Faith will leads us into the relationship with God and to drive us to bear fruits.

Question Five: What are the fruits that we are to bear?

- Strength
- Joy
- Peace
- Power
- Blessing
- Wisdom
- Knowledge
- Patience
- Fruits of the Spirit – Galatians 5:22-23

You should notice that your answers are similar to question 1. Indeed, that what we receive from the source should reflect types of our fruits that we bear.

Question Six: Looking back in your life for last 5-15 years, has your relationship with God grown in those years? If so, how much?

- Answers will vary, try to probe so you can create better discussion.

Question Seven: Where are you in your walk with God? (Don't ask them to tell you, but get them to think) Where do you want to be in next 6 months? What do you need to do to reach there?

Question Eight: What are some daily habits that you can do to nurture your relationship with God, this week? Get specific goals.

- Set aside a prayer time
- Decide to fast a certain amount
- Set aside a time for Bible study

Conclusion:

To grow a successful garden, you must work on it daily such as: planting, watering, plowing, weeding, fertilizing, and pruning. So is our relationship with God. Paul said, "I die daily." (I Corinthians 15:31) He walked with God daily not just Sunday. It requires daily walk with God. We must pray daily. We must read the Bible daily. We must rededicate our lives daily. We must spiritually discipline ourselves daily. You as a Christian should have a specific daily habits to improve and deepen your relationship with God such as: I will fast every Monday, and pray 20 minutes in the morning. By doing so, one day at a time, we can continue grow our relationship with God.

Synopsis:

You are todays church! Your talents and abilities are in high demand now and should be utilised for the Kingdom now, not later! However it takes commitment to be a success and not just any commitment but one that goes all the way! There are many different areas that we can choose or be called to to impact the Kingdom of God, which will you choose?

Ice-Breaker:

- **Here's a $100 bill, and assume I will hand it to you. What would you do with it?**
- **Now, if I restrict you to only using it to glorify God, what would you do?**

Introduction:
In Matthew 25:14-30, Jesus gives the well-known parable of servants and talents. What is the moral of this story? As a Christian, you are responsible to utilize your own talents to glorify God. What are you doing with your talents, skills, knowledge, ideas, and abilities? What has God given you as your talents and skills? Are you using them? Is your master pleased with the way you are utilizing what He has given to you? One of your purposes as a Christian is to build the kingdom of God by utilizing your talents. In the United States, 85% of Christians backslide when they are in your age group. However, a leading youth ministry magazine, Group, concludes that young people who are involved and serving in their local church are less likely to backslide. When God chose you to be a His child, He also called you to serve. Today, let's ask ourselves a question, "What are we doing for God with what we have?"

Question One: What can we do to build and be involved in the Kingdom of God?

- Teach Sunday School
- Intercessory Prayer
- Witness
- Music Ministry
- Involvement in ministries (youth, children, prison, nursing home, homeless, bus/trans portation, etc) – whatever your church has open to you

Question Two: What did Moses accomplish as the leader of Israelites?

- Stood up against Pharaoh
- Led exodus of several million people
- Passed through the Red Sea
- Fed and took care of them daily
- Ten Commandments
- Founder of Jewish religion, culture, and law

Question Three: How did Moses reach such a great faith to accomplish these profound things in his life?

- The key is serious commitment
- His walk with God
- The help of leaders around him

Question Four: In Exodus 3 and 4 we find Moses arguing with God about his role in the Kingdom. What was Gods response?

- God showed Moses how he was already equipped to accomplish the task, then Moses realized that abilities are from God and the Lord was on his side. This realization led Moses to be fully committed to his calling.

Question Five: Read **Exodus 32:11-14**. How serious was Moses commitment?

- Moses prayed that God would forgive the people even when God said He would make a nation from Moses

- Moses in the stead of God severely chastised the people by grounding up the calf and mixing it in their water to drink. He was committed to leading them.

Question Six: Let's read **Exodus 4:1 - 5** to find out what God told Moses regarding to do things for the Kingdom of God.

- God took what Moses already had - a staff
- When you are committed, God will take what you already possess and He will use you in His way. Just put your life into His hands.

Question Seven: So, what's next after the commitment?

- Fulfilling your calling now
- Following where God leads

Question Eight: What are your talents, skills, knowledge, ideas, and abilities? (If you have time, let this be an open discussion. If your church already has a talent survey, use your church's survey. Survey activity can be a take-home activity if the time does not allow.)

Conclusion:

In any career path/profession you choose in life, there are always three steps.

- **Step 1: commitment**
- **Step 2: training**
- **Step 3: execution/practice/apply**

Serving God is the same way. We must first make a commitment. All of you are capable of making a great impact in the kingdom of God, and becoming a great kingdom builder. It is God's desire that everyone build the Kingdom. However, some will choose to bury the talent their Master has trusted the with. What's the difference? Commitment! Without commitment Moses could not fulfill his calling. Without commitment, you can not fulfill your calling. I'm not talking about being a preacher, I'm talking about being a Christian□being a Kingdom Builder. Some may tell you that you are the future of this church. No way, you are Today's church.

- **Where does the commitment begin? In the heart.**
- **Your commitment will be tested. Commitment requires action.**
- **Commitment will:**
- **Help you to resist opposition**
- **Help you to overcome difficulties**
- **Encourage you to excel**

Synopsis:

God ordained the family. It is the very first institution, and it is the fabric of society. Our relationship within our families is a source of strength, safety and encouragement. We should feel free to express ourselves within our family, to be ourselves always, but definitely with our family and to communicate effectively and open with our family. Above all, our family should be dedicated to God.

Ice-Breaker:

Does anyone have any strange family traditions? Can be holiday related or non-holiday related.

What is your happiest memory with your family? Christmas as a child, vacation trip etc...

Introduction:

Our family is such an important institution. The very fabric of our society is traced all the way down to our families. The family is the fabric of the church, the church is the fabric of society and our societies are what make our country great! It's important that we maintain a proper relationship with our family as they are a source of encouragement, strength and a sanctuary for us. Our family can provide so much happiness and so many fond memories that can sustain us and keep us on the right path. They can also form the pattern in which you raise your own family some day, with the same traditions and places to visit etc...Let's explore the topic of family relationships a little more.

Question One: What do you feel are the most important aspects of a family?

- Trust
- Love
- Safety

Question Two: As young adults, how does your relationship with you parents change from childhood to now?

- Even though you're older, you still must respect and honor them
- Their advice should be taken into account still
- The level and depth of communication can change and develop

Question Three: What determines family to you?

- Someone you trust and are very close to
- Someone who lives with you but may not be born of the same family
- Someone who shares the same beliefs and values as you do

Question Four: Read **Ephesians 3:15**. If the whole family in heaven and earth is named after Jesus, what does that reveal to us about the family?

- If we have His name, we should live like He wants us to
- We should represent His name well, bring Him honor
- God has a family as well, you and I. We are important to God so a family is as well

Question Five: What are some ways you can ruin or harm your relationship with your family?

- Deception or dishonesty
- Saying mean or hurtful things to them or about them
- Not spending time with them

Question Six: Read **Joshua 24:15**. Joshua made a stand and determined that his family was going to serve God. How can you accomplish this?

- Pray and fast with the family, a family time of prayer and fasting
- A weekly bible study with just the family
- Attending church as often as possible and staying involved as much as possible

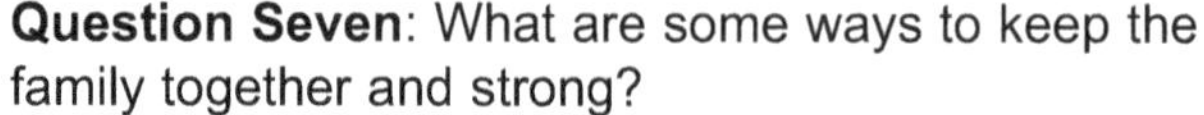

Question Seven: What are some ways to keep the family together and strong?

- Spend time together often, not just during the holidays
- Plan family get-aways even if its just for a day or two
- Determine to always have an open communication amongst each other, maintain honesty and trust with one another

Question Eight:We have certain rights, roles and responsibilities in our families. Read **Ephesians 2:19**. What rights and responsibilities do members of God's family have?

- The Promises of the Word of God belong to us
- The responsibilities to witness and work for His Kingdom
- The role of sons and daughters, honoring our Father God and Mother Church

Conclusion:

The family institution is important as we have seen. It's important that our relationship with our family is right as our roles change. When we are children, our role should be to honor our mother and father and to obey and learn but to also have fun, create memories and enjoy the safe and loving environment that a family is supposed to provide us. When we grow into adults and have our own family the Bible gives us further direction on how to fulfill those roles. We also have our role in God's family. We should always strive to maintain a healthy and positive relationship with our family. These are the people we should be able to trust and expect love and encouragement from, but sometimes it's the people who can hurt us the most. That's why it's important for our families to be submitted to God, a Godly family is a perfect family regardless of its shortcomings.

A Friend Indeed

Synopsis:

Our friendships can be some of the most deep and meaningful relationships in our lives. We invest so much time, energy and love in our friendships and as a result are blessed tremendously. There are many biblical examples of what a true friendship should be like and examples of what true friends are. It's also important to make sure we're friends with the right people; a friendship should be mutually beneficial.

Ice-Breaker:

- **Can you name some of the most famous pairs of friends throughout the Bible? (David and Jonathan, Paul and Barnabas etc)**
- **Did you have a "best friend" growing up? Are you still that close?**

Introduction:

God desires us to have close relationships. He gave us companions all the way back in Genesis and we see the term friendship explained and displayed throughout the Bible. It's important to God that we have someone with us for several reasons. To fight together, laugh together, work together but also to help us in our times of trouble, to encourage us and lift us up. What are the requirements for a Godly friendship? Does God care who we are friends with? Let's explore the topic of friendship a little more.

Question One: If you had to define friendship using only one word, what would you define it as?

- Love
- Loyalty
- Caring

Question Two:Read **Proverbs 18:24**. How can you show yourself to be friendly?

- Smile when looking at people
- Listen intently when they are talking to you
- Love them at all times, encourage when they need it

Question Three: What aspects do you look for most in a friend?

- Sense of humor
- Honesty
- Acceptance

Question Four: Read **John 15:13**. Why do you think the aspect of sacrifice is important in a friendship?

- Friends should be willing to sacrifice for each other, a give and take relationship
- Jesus equated this with love so if we love our friends this is an important attitude for us to have

Question Five: The story of David and Jonathan illustrates several key elements of friendship. Summarize the story found in **I Samuel 18 – 20** or have them read some key verses. What elements of true friendship can we see displayed?

- Dependability
- They will stand up for you
- They will give and sacrifice for you

Question Six: Read **II Corin. 2:14**. Why does the Bible warn us against friendships with unbelievers?

- They can lead us down the wrong paths
- We can be influenced by their lifestyle and hurt our walk with God
- They may be using us instead of really loving us

Question Seven: In order for our relationship with God to grow, sometimes we need to break off some bad friendships, how do you do that?

- Don't just cut off communication; explain your reasons, if they were truly your friends it may really hurt them if you just stop talk ing, plus you don't want to burn a bridge you may need to cross someday to be a witness

- Wean yourself off their company; tell them you'd like to spend more time praying and drawing closer to God, ask if they'd like to as well, if they're interested you may help them, if not they're making the decision, not you.

- Pray for God's direction and talk to your Pastor about it.

Question Eight:The most important friendship you will ever have is your relationship with Jesus. What are some of the ways you can develop that?

- Prayer and fasting!
- Devoting your time to reading His Word
- Witnessing and working for His Kingdom

Conclusion:

Our walk with God should be the most important thing in our life. His guidance, His love and His warmth will draw a number of people to your side but it can also repel those who are rebelling against it. Above all else, our friendship with Jesus should be cultivated most. Sometimes to do that you have to let go of some things in this world and that includes some friends who may be holding you back. While it is a hard and painful thing to do, the rewards far outweigh the pain. Your wayward friend may respect your decision and that could be the witness they need to start their own relationship with God. You should never be afraid to do the right thing! A friend is such an awesome and wonderful thing to have. All the fun, laughter, memories and love are well worth the effort that goes in to maintaining one, just be sure we're maintaining the right ones! Lastly, remember that there's no greater love than to lay down your life for your friends. Jesus was the greatest example of a friend; spend some time this week getting to know Him a little more. You just might learn how to be a better friend as well as a better Christian.

Synopsis:

Most of this age group is either already on the path to marriage or seriously considering it. If not now, then sometime in the near future the word marriage will become a reality. It's important to understand what true biblical love is, some of the pitfalls and dangers that lead to an unsuccessful marriage as well as some of the things to ask yourself before asking "the" question.

Ice-Breaker:

- **When you were younger, how old did you think you would be when you got married?**
- **How many of you are thinking about getting married or having a serious relationship with the purpose of getting married in the not too distant future? If so, how long until?**

Introduction:

Most young adults and college/career aged adults plan on getting married or at least having a serious relationship in their future. Many are already at that stage. The prospect of marriage and family is a real possibility and a desire for many at this age. The average age for marriage in the United States is: males - 25.9 years old and females - 24.6 years old. Therefore, at your age, it is very natural to turn your thoughts toward marriage and the choosing of your mate. The next few years will be crucial in your decision-making process. That's why today we are going to discuss true love beyond just movie-flick romance or flings. We are going to look at true love that goes beyond your emotions.

Question One: What causes some romantic relationships to succeed and others to fail?

- Wrong motives/reasons to get married
- Unbalanced
- God
- Misunderstanding or luck of patient to understand

Question Two: What does the Bible say about romantic/marriage relationship?

- Read Ephesians 5:22-25
- Much like the relationship between the church and God

Question Three: The Bible clearly talks about how we ought to love God. Read **Mark 12:29 – 30**. What does it say about loving God?

- Heart
- Soul
- Mind
- Strength

Question Four: What does it mean to love someone with all of your heart, soul, mind and strength?

- Heart = emotional
- Soul = spiritual / unity (Philippians 2:2)
- Mind = intellectual
- Strength = physical

Question Five: What is the purpose of marriage?

- Genesis 1:27-28
- A couple with true love should support each other to add value to the other's career, spiritual walk, and social status.
- Furthermore, true companionship must create synergy, which means, "1 + 1 = 3." In other words, synergy is when two individuals together create more than what they could create individually. As the companionship of church and Christ creates great revival, the companionship of man and woman should create productive results for their spiritual and secular life.

Question Six: Let's Read **John 15:13** and find one of key ingredients of successful relationship?

- Total commitment
- Dedication
- Giving
- Sacrificial Lifestyle

Question Seven: Christ loves the church unconditionally. What does it mean to love someone unconditionally?

- Romans 8:38-39
- 1 Corinthians 13:4-8

Question Eight: If you are currently in a romantic relationship, think of these 8 powerful questions.

- Am I in love my partner emotionally?
- Do I have a spiritual unity with my partner?
- Does our relationship make sense?
- Am I physically attractive to my partner?
- Does our relationship have positive impacts in our career?
- Are we doing more for the kingdom of God together?
- How committed and dedicated are we to each other?
- Do I love this person 'till death us do apart?

Conclusion:

These elements are the essential ingredients of true love. In God's love, and in His expectation of our love to Him, we can clearly see these elements demonstrated. Thus, before making the vow, couples must thoroughly analyze their relationship in relation to these elements of true love. With a clear understanding and knowledge of true biblical love, couples should guide themselves to discover if their feelings are "true love" or it is just another "romance." In America today, over 50% of marriages end in divorce. This is a real dilemma. For Christians, real thought and prayerful planning must go into the decision to marry. Nobody likes talking about divorce and the pains it can cause, but everything that can be done by us on the front end to prevent a divorce, must be done.

Synopsis:

We will all interact with our non-believing peers at some point throughout our day and those interactions can be some of the most important moments in their day and ours. We need to demonstrate the Love of God through our actions, our words and our lifestyle. We are to reflect Jesus, not ourselves. At the same time we must guard ourselves against the influences they bring to us and ultimately pray without ceasing for God to use us in our relationships.

Ice-Breaker:

- **How many here are on Facebook?**
- **How many friends do you have there? In church and not in church?**

Introduction:

Everyday we interact with people, all kinds of people. From those who believe and walk as you do to those who are the furthest from it. We even walk among those who are watching and waiting for us to fail and slip up. Yet everyday we have relationships with these people. Via conversations, texts, social media, face to face interactions etc....and your relationships with these people are very important. None so important as those who do not yet have the relationship and experience with God that the Bible tells us about. Your relationships and how you conduct yourself in these interactions play a very important role in their eternal destination! Let's explore this topic further.

Question One: Read **Proverbs 18:21**. What does this have to do with our lesson?

- Our communication is important and can either lead to death or life
- The way we interact with unbelievers can influence whether or not they decide to live for God
- A fruit comes from our communication and we must inevitably eat of it, whether it is positive and a good fruit or negative and a bad one, we will eat it.

Question Two: What's the difference between being transformed and being conformed? Which should we strive for others to be?

- Conforming means to act more like something, be like what someone else expects us to be
- Transformed changes the very nature of who we are, a new and different person
- Transformed! Our goal should be for Jesus to transform our unbelieving peers into new creatures in Christ.

Question Three: When you hear the phrase "Soul Winner" what does that really mean to you?

- A person who has lead someone to salvation
- A person who disciples another person
- A person who lives in such a way as to inspire others to live for God

Question Four: What are some of the dangers in having a relationship with unbelievers?

- We can be negatively impacted, start to compromise our beliefs
- We will start to be conformed to what they want, their influence can overwhelm our witness if we aren't strong enough and prayerful
- We can lose sight of the fact that they are indeed lost, good people yes, but ultimately still without Jesus.

Question Five: What are some ways that you can live a soul-winning relationship with your peers?

- Have positive conversations with others and give God the glory, you don't have to be overbearing with it but let it be known the good things that God has done
- Listen to others and do not criticize what they believe when it differs from you. Go to the Scripture.
- LOVE THEM. People don't care how much you know until they know how much you care! Being there for them in tough times can open doors for you to share your testimony and the Word of God.

Question Six: Jesus said that by our fruit, others will know that we are His disciples. Read **Galatians 5:22**. How can you show this fruit in your relationship with your peers?

- Have each student pick a fruit and give an example of how to show it.
- Ex. Joy: Always have a smile when interacting with them, let them see the Joy of the Lord in your life.
- Ex. Peace: Others often have trails and troubles and so do we, but we have the peace that passes all understanding, let them know what you're going through as well, but that God is with you and His peace abides etc…

Question Seven: What's the difference between interaction and fellowship with our lost peers?

- Fellowship is deeper than interaction, you take part in things together, more of a bond, a sharing of self and giving to one another
- Fellowship requires more time to be spent, we can fellowship with believers but with unbelievers fellowship can be dangerous if not kept carefully
- Interactions are going to come whether we choose to or not, we will have conversations and dealings with others, however fellowship is a matter of choice, willful desire etc…

Question Eight: Read **Ephesians 5:11-17**. How can we walk circumspectly and redeem the time?

- Make the best use of our time in this world, plan to reach others every day!
- Think about how you can impact someone you know you will see today, how can you reach them?
- The Will of God is that none should perish, so decide to be a soul-winner and reach for the lost.

Conclusion:

Jesus said that we are the light and salt of the world and that we cannot hide our light. Jesus said that we are in this world but we are not of this world meaning we are in it, we will have to meet these people and the forces of darkness head on. We are the ones He has chosen to reach this world and combat the spiritual wickedness of our day. However, we are not of this world, meaning we cannot allow ourselves to be contaminated or brought down by these people and principalities. We must learn to love, and truly love the people we interact with everyday. One of the truest sayings you will ever learn is that "love demands a response." It is expected that you will have relationships with your unbelieving peers, its part of being in the world. It's very different to actively seek fellowship with an unbeliever, that's part of not being of this world. Our goal is not to be conformed to this world but to be transformed and lead others to the same experience. Our conversations, our actions, our ethics, our lifestyle all shout to the world and our peers what we stand for and what we really believe which is why we must put on Christ and manifest the fruit of the Spirit in our life. Realize that everyday and in every place you go and in every interaction you have with people, YOU are at that moment God's ambassador to a lost world. Even when you're not directly interacting with others, you are still being watched. Preach the Gospel, and if necessary, use words!

Synopsis:

Giving is a heart condition. The way we give is also a good indicator of our maturity and our faith. We must remember that God owns everything and gives to us everything we have. When a need in the Kingdom arises, His money needs to be allocated to that need. Now it becomes a trust issue with God. Do we trust Him to still be our provider when asked to give His money to an area of His Kingdom in need?

Ice-Breaker:

What is the most money you've ever spent at one time, or on one thing?

Does anyone here have any investments like stocks or bonds? How are they doing?

Introduction:

Few, if any of us, would be classified as "free-givers" by nature. Think about it... It is not always a good feeling to give away something you have worked hard to earn. None of us would naturally consider approaching our boss and asking him to give our hourly pay to our co-workers. No, we just are not wired that way. We want what is rightfully ours. In this day and age, there are some situations where giving is attractive to our flesh. We are especially fond of giving when we think we will reap a positive return for our gift. Some give huge sums of money to have their names placed on buildings or monuments. Some give gifts with strings attached. "I will give as long as I get this or that treatment or reward in return". To truly be a "giver" according to God's plan, though, we have to have a heart that is right with God. Let's look into God's Word and see what He says about this "giving" heart condition...

Question One: What is the difference between an Offering and Sacrifice?

- A sacrifice can be painful…giving till it hurts
- A sacrifice can mean going above the normal to the point it really effects us
- An offering you kind of expect to give, a sacrifice is something bigger and perhaps sometimes unexpected

Question Two: Read **Matthew 6:19-21**. What does this verse tell us?

- We should not devote ourselves to hoarding up money or the treasures of this world as they will all fade away and be destroyed
- Whatever we deem to be treasure, our heart will be there with it
- If we attach ourselves to physical things we will only be disappointed because it will all eventually be destroyed or stolen

Question Three: Spending too much can affect our giving, what about saving or being too frugal? How can that affect our giving?

- We can habitually hoard up our finances to the point we don't spend or give
- Could lead to more giving if you have saved it to give etc

Question Four: What are some areas you feel are really important to give to?

- World Missions
- Outreach
- Sheaves for Christ

Question Five: Read **Deut.15:10.** What does this verse mean to you?

- God wants us to be happy about giving
- God will bless us if we give
- If there is a need, we shouldn't give begrudgingly but gladly

Question Six: Some have said that Giving is the highest form of worship. Do you think this is true? Why or why not?

- It's a trust issue. Can sometimes be easy to trust God with our soul since we don't really see it or can touch it, but when it comes to "our" money, it's a little harder to let it go, trust that it's the thing to do
- We are paid for our time, in essence, our life. We sell our lives a portion of the day for a wage and to us that money represents a portion of our life we've sold, now when we give to God, its not just our money but really a piece of our lives

Question Seven: What are some of the hindrances to giving an offering or a sacrificial offering?

- Don't feel like you can afford it
- Thinking what you can give really wouldn't help much, count on others who can give more
- Lack of sensitivity to the Spirit when prompted to give

Question Eight: Read **Malachi 3:8-11**. What does this verse mean to our discussion?

- Not giving God back His tenth and giving in offerings is equivalent to stealing from God
- God is serious and sets a high priority on giving, enough to call it stealing when not done
- Gods blessing will be on those who do give and He will protect their income

Conclusion:

Giving really is a heart condition. The Bible says we are to be cheerful givers! We should be honored that God has trusted us enough with His finances to ask us to give so He can give back to us even more. Giving to God is the best investment you could ever make. If our hearts are in tune with God, our giving will be as well. If there are trust issues or a lacking of faith or maturity in our walk with God, it will usually manifest itself in our giving. We must be careful or we will deceive ourselves. We must remember, everything belongs to God and all that we "have" He has given us. To keep it back and say you need it more is awfully presumptuous and haughty considering He is the one who both gives....and takes away. There are so many wonderful areas in the Kingdom of God that we can be a blessing to, from giving to Missionaries who are reaching the world with the Gospel to our own local Outreach programs or food banks helping others right here at home. Giving is an essential and awesome aspect of living for God!

Synopsis:

There are thousands of potential career choices in this world and the education that we pursue will play a great role in determining this. We should try to keep our options open and seek the Will of God for our life when making such an important decision because there are potential pitfalls in secular universities and Bible colleges as well. Ultimately it pays to think ahead, and of course, pray and fast!

Ice-Breaker:

- **Think back to when you were a child, what did you want to be when you grew up?**
- **Now compare that idea to where you are currently or the direction you are headed, i.e. courses enrolled in, work history etc...are you on the same track? Why or why not? What is the difference between then and now?**

Introduction:

At this point in your lives many of you have either decided, or started the process of deciding how you're going to make a living the rest of your life. Most people choose their educational path by deciding what kind of work they want to do later in life. Before beginning training then, it is important for one to decide which kind of career one desires. Not everyone is ready at this stage to commit to one career. If unsure, it may help to have a time of soul searching through reading the Word, praying and fasting. It may help to remember these things:

a. Young adults can redo whatever decisions they make. It is early in life.
b. Do not be afraid to try or consider many options.
c. College majors may not directly reflect future careers.
d. Happiness is more important than a huge salary.

Question One: What should be taken into account when considering a career?

- Is it God's Perfect Will?
- Is it in demand or on the decline?
- Is this particular field already overcrowded and/or saturated?
- What education or training do I need?
- What's the average starting salary and/or benefits?

Question Two: Education often determines the career we choose, and vice-versa, but other than that what's the purpose of getting an education or undergoing the necessary training?

- Gaining skills
- Increasing knowledge
- Gaining discipline
- Personal development

Question Three: What does the phrase "Success is determined by character" mean to you?

- A good education and/or talent does not always equal out to a successful career.
- The character of a man or woman is more valuable in the long run than just an education.
- A successful life must be Christ-Centered, for only then will one's character stand the test of time and temptations.

Question Four: While getting your education or training, what are some of the dangers involved for a Christian attending a secular institution?

- Classes you "need" only available during service times
- Unprepared for peer pressure and temptations lurking to get you to compromise

Question Five: How do you avoid or overcome the dangers or pitfalls you mentioned?

- Seek ye first the Kingdom of God
- Prayer, fasting, commitment to the Word of God
- A strong foundation in the Word will help you withstand any form of doctrine contrary to the Bible

Question Six: We've talked about careers and educations in a secular world, but what of the church? What are your thoughts on the ministry and Bible Colleges?

- A called profession, not a chosen one
- Unstable or insecure, not fiscally wise seemingly
- Write down some of their thoughts to discuss further

Question Seven: Read Psalm 103. What does this passage of scripture tell us about "working for God?" What are some of the other benefits you think come with the work of God?

- God has great benefits! Not just for those in the ministry but for all His children!
- Seeing the miraculous perhaps more often than the typical saint.
- Greater respect.
- Is there a difference in the benefits for the saint and for the ministry?

Question Eight:Our careers can often overwhelm or overshadow other aspects of life. What are some of the most important things in life aside from your job?

- Family
- Church
- Vacation time
- Serving others

Conclusion:

Many of us here in this room have either already decided on a career path or will soon decide and it's one of the most important decisions you will ever make. Take some time to prayerfully consider the many fields of choice available. Research and use the tools and tests available to aide you in this decision. Keep the main thing the main thing, as in always keep God first, regardless of our school schedule or job hours. Prayerfully consider a life in the ministry, if God has called you, nothing else will satisfy you. Just make sure that the calling is of God and then make full proof of your ministry. Overall make sure that whatever your chosen career is that it doesn't take over your life. God did not create us to work 80 hours a week and sleep when we are dead. Jesus came that we might have life and have it more abundantly! Don't let your life revolve around your job but make sure your job revolves around your life that's hopefully been given to God. Read Matthew 6:33. Whether you've chosen a secular career or you've answered the call to ministry you must always seek first His Kingdom and then your own and all the things we desire will be added unto you. Close with Psalm 37:3-6.

The Financial Plan

Synopsis:

A lack of self discipline usually will manifest itself in the area of our finances but will also affect our spiritual life as well. As Christians we should learn how to plan! Plan with the future in mind, plan to be a part of Gods plan and trust that He knows best. We also need to realize the importance of Giving and how that plays into our finances being blessed, not taken away.

Ice-Breaker:

- **Anyone here a shopaholic?**
- **How many credit cards do you have or have access to?**

Introduction:

There are many Christians that argue about whether it is biblical to plan finances. Those who argue against planning misunderstand what God says about finances. There are those who argue that God expects us to rely on Him for everything instead of planning. Others create plans so inflexible that they can no longer respond to God's leading. Clearly the answer lies somewhere in between. God is an orderly provider. The physical world is not chaotic; it is orderly and well-planned. Atoms stay together because God so ordered them. Finances are just another aspect of the Christian's life that God wants to manage. If we are stewards and God is the owner, we must seek His wisdom. Therefore we must go to God's Word for our plans. Let's explore this topic further.

Question One: What are some ways a Christian can be financially undisciplined? Why do you think that is?

- Buying things they don't really need, impulse buying etc
- Not paying their bills, shopping instead
- Not giving, using the money for things they want, selfishness

Question Two: When you hear the word Steward, what does that mean to you?

- Money-manager
- Caretaker
- A person with whom authority has been left with while the master is away

Question Three: Read **Luke 16:10-12.** What does this verse tell us about finances?

- If we misuse the little money we have we won't be trusted with more
- If we can't learn to correctly use worldly wealth we won't be trusted with true riches
- If we are not a good steward of Gods things there will be little else for us to worry about in our own lives

Question Four: It's often been said that money is the root of all evil. Read **I Timothy 6:10**. What does the scripture say about money?

- Money isn't evil but the love of it is
- It can cause people to lose their relationship with God
- It can bring many sorrows

Question Five: What ways can a Christian be financially disciplined?

- Set up a budget and follow it
- Give always and always follow the Lord on giving
- Limit your amount of debt to finances ratio

Question Six: Read **Matthew 6:24**. What does this verse tell us about our finances?

- That we will either serve God or our finances, not both
- Our finances, or money, can negatively impact our walk with God
- If we serve God, our finances must also serve Him

Question Seven: Read **I Timothy 6:6**. How does this verse play into our discussion?

- We should be content with what God has given us and learn to plan with it
- Being wise and content with our finances is Godly
- Being content with what we have can discipline us to be better stewards

Question Eight: Aside from the necessary areas of a budget like Rent, Insurance, Giving etc…what else should be included?

- Savings
- Entertainment
- Medical

Conclusion:

The Bible makes clear in several places that God owns it all! What we have He has given to us. In that sense we truly are stewards of His finances, not owners of ours. We should learn to use the finances He has provided wisely. We must set a plan and use that plan, we should be disciplined in our spending and follow a budget. We should also ensure that Giving is a high priority for our finances. After all, the money belongs to Him and if His Kingdom requires it for something it should be no question as to whether we should give it or not. God has promised to always provide for us and it becomes a matter of trust and faith if our giving is not according to His Word and Will. Learn to trust God in what He has given you to take care of, after all our goal is hear the words "well done, thou good and faithful servant."

Out of Bounds!

Synopsis:

Since we are God's Steward we should strive to use God's money wisely. We will ask some questions to better understand what a budget is and why it is important in our lives and important to God!

Ice-Breaker:

- **In playing any kind of game or activity do you remember there being an "Out of bounds" in it? What was the purpose of that?**
- **How many of you have ever been truly broke? No money at all or not enough to really do anything...what did that feel like?**

Introduction:

Since God is our provider, He is the one who gives us our jobs or provisions and therefore since He owns everything, realistically all the money belongs to Him. So it would make since that God is interested in how we spend the money He allots to us. Obviously we want to use His money wisely when we finally realize that it is indeed His money. One of the wisest and proven methods in being a faithful steward is to work off of and live off of a budget! Let's dig a little deeper into this subject.

Question One: What exactly is a budget first off?

- An allotment of monies into certain categories of expenses in our life designed to keep us within a certain range
- A tool used to help us live within our means
- A boundary!

Question Two: Why is a budget sometimes considered a boundary?

- It shows us just how far we can safely go
- A boundary keeps us within a certain space, a budget does the same thing for our finances
- Outside the boundary there are no guarantees, outside our budget there is danger as well

Question Three: It has often been said that Jesus spoke of money more than just about anything else. Why do you think that is?

- Jesus realized the dangers in the peoples love for it
- Jesus realized that if people were financially disciplined it would help them to be spiritually disciplined
- Money is sometimes the most difficult and personal thing for people to deal with so Jesus spoke on it more.

Question Four:If you got to choose how much money you made a year, what would you choose? Why?

- Amounts will differ but the "why" is what's important.

Question Five: If you got to choose how much money you made a year, what would you choose? Why?

- More money than you know what to do with
- Having enough money to pay all your bills, give as much as you would like or is needed to the church and still have a little extra
- Jesus' was perhaps to be able to provide for all the needs of His people (as if He couldn't!)

Question Six: Thinking about a budget, what are some things you spend your money on weekly?

- Food
- Gas
- Entertainment

Question Seven: What are some things that you deem absolutely necessary in your life?

- Giving
- Car
- Phone etc…answers will vary

Question Eight: Read **Luke 19:11-27**. What do you think Jesus is trying to teach us?

- The way we use what He trusts us with is important
- Using His money unwisely could be a heaven or hell issue
- To those who use it wisely, more will be added, to those who do not what they have will be taken away

Conclusion:

Money is simply a tool - a tool to acquire services and possessions for our satisfaction and necessities. A tool's performance, though, is based on its operator, the one using the tool. Take the hammer, for instance. With this, I can build houses, furniture, etc., but I can also use it to destroy. It is essentially up to me, the operator, and my particular skill in using this object. In the same sense, you can also use your money as a tool of construction or destruction. If you learn to take charge of your money, you will become very successful at it. If you misuse it, you can very possibly destroy your life. You must be in charge. You must take responsibility. Using a budget is using the tool wisely. Being financially undisciplined however can be very destructive both to your physical well being and your spiritual. Take some time and set up a budget for yourself if you haven't already done one and do your best to stick to it, remember, using money wisely can end up leading you to more!

Synopsis:

Debt is a serious issue and one that is plaguing many young people today due to a lack of knowledge! Understanding what debt is, both good and bad, is key to establishing a sound financial future. Getting out of bad debt can be extremely difficult and costly, but ultimately worth while.

Ice-Breaker:

- **Has anyone here ever had to declare Bankruptcy in Monopoly? What happened?**
- **If you had no debt at all, how much money do you think you could save or invest or give?**

Introduction:

As the issue of debt becomes an increasing concern, young adults must decide early not to fall into the trap to which so many have succumbed. Young Americans ages 24 to 34 now have the second highest rate of bankruptcy, just after those aged 35 to 44 ("Generation Broke: Growth of Debt Among Young Americans"). Debt and spending habits created as young adults will often determine their financial future for years to come. Therefore, it is vitally important to learn the secrets of not getting into debt in the first place. For those who already find themselves in debt, it's important to learn the answer to becoming debt-free. We will discuss a little of both topics today.

Question One: Read **Proverbs 22:7** and **Romans 13:8**. What does the Bible say about debt?

- The borrower is a SLAVE to the lender
- We should owe no man anything
- Debt happens, but we should avoid it

Question Two: What are some steps to take to keep us debt free?

- Spend less than you make, live off a budget
- Don't use credit cards, if you can't pay for it in cash you don't need it
- Set up an emergency savings fund just in case you lose your job or have a medical need or other "true" emergency

Question Three: What if we're already in debt, how do we get out?

- Again, establish a budget and work it!
- Start paying it off. List what you have and pay the minimum amounts on all but the first one, then with whatever is left "attack" the first one till it's paid off and then go to the next
- Stop spending on credit!

Question Four:Some people mistakenly think that "things" make us happy. What are some of the dangers of materialism?

- It can lead you into debt!
- It hurts your walk with God
- Anything that can hurt you spiritually can eventually lead to physical and mental hurt as well

Question Five: What are some things that truly make us happy?

- Our family and friends
- Our walk with God
- Enjoying life in general

Question Six: If we are spending more than we make, what can we do to change?

- Change our perspective, things we had to have we no longer see as important
- Ask for help, find a friend or family member and ask them to keep you accountable
- Cut up your credit cards

Question Seven: Think about your life and spending habits, if you had to, what areas could you sacrifice to cut back on spending?

- Going out to eat
- Shopping for clothes or shoes
- Changing cell phone plans to a lower one

Question Eight: Read **Deut. 28:1,12**. What do these verses tell us about our discussion?

- God will bless us
- God wants us to be a lender, not a borrower
- The pre-requisite is that we must diligently obey our Lord!

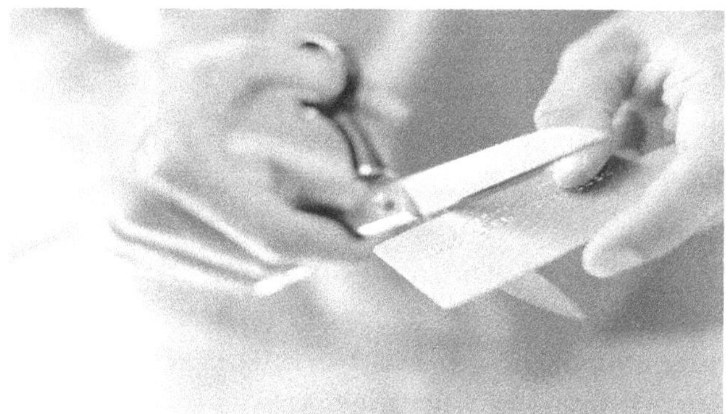

Conclusion:

The bottom line on debt is that it comes from buying things that we don't have the money to pay for. In our society, we are well accustomed to "buy it now and pay later." Yet it is this very practice that gets us into trouble. Don't fall into the same trap as the majority of young adults in America. Learn to enjoy the freedom of being debt free. Zig Ziglar says, "If you aim at nothing, you will hit it every time." Be in the minority and make a plan now to live free from debt. Don't get caught up in the rush for "things" which can only provide fleeting happiness. Instead, invest in the things of God and there you will find true joy, contentment, peace and happiness!

Synopsis:

Financial ethics is a very important topic in our world, especially as of late. America is only just now peeking its head out of the Great Recession and some still think we have a ways to go before we're out of the woods. As Christians we should always make sound and ethical decisions. We need to ask ourselves who makes the rules – God or man? Then follow those rules to the best of our abilities.

Ice-Breaker:

- **Can you describe some recent examples of unethical behavior that's been in our headlines the last few years?**
- **Is it ever ok to steal? Under what circumstance and why?**

Introduction:

Lack of ethics in finance is one of the primary factors which led to the fall of Wall Street and the near collapse of the U.S. economy in September and October of 2008. It precipitated the worst recession since the Great Depression. Many large banking and insurance firms failed. Small business failed as well, including small banks that had made risky loans. The result was inevitable. When companies act unethically they are doomed to failure. As Christians, whether we own our own business or just work for someone else's business, we should be examples of ethical behavior. When we consider ethics in financial matters, we must consider who makes the rules – God or man? This question is what the issue of ethics is all about. Either there is a supernatural source for what is morally right, absolute, universal standard that is beyond ourselves, i.e. God, or we are left to ourselves to figure out what is right and wrong, if we can even agree that there is a right and a wrong. Let's explore this topic further.

Question One: What are some other words for Ethics?

- Morals
- Principles/Values
- Convictions

Question Two: Read **Proverbs 23:19**. What does this verse add to our discussion?

- We should be careful how we live because others are watching
- We should use wisdom in our life choices and the way we work
- Our heart should be guided by wisdom as we navigate our world

Question Three: What would you do if your company or your boss took a turn against your ethical stance or asked you to?

- Talk with the boss and explain your convictions/values and why you cannot do what they ask.
- Look for some sort of alternative or level ground but never compromise.
- If it persists, you may need to find a new job or seek some other resolution

Question Four: Read **Deut. 25:13-15**. What does this verse tell us about ethics?

- We should give the full purchase in exchange for a fair payment
- Full quality for what is paid for – don't cheat!
- Give a full days work for a full days pay, or vice versa

Question Five: Read **Romans 12:17**. What does this scripture add to our discussion?

- We should be honest and good even when others are not
- We should always do what's right
- Our standards should be higher than others

Question Six: In dealing with people you will at some point cross hairs with someone, how are we supposed to react? What ethical guidelines can help us?

- Think of the Golden Rule, treat others the way we want to be treated
- Think of Jesus and the red letters, turn the other cheek!
- Forgive them and forgive them and forgive them, 70 times 7 etc

Question Seven: Do you think it's possible to succeed in our capitalist market which seeks its own first and still be ethically sound? Why or why not?

- Yes, God will bless our business. If we take care of God's business He will take care of ours....
- Yes, There are numerous companies doing well who also uphold ethical guidelines (Servicemaster, Chik-Fil-A etc...)
- Perhaps, but what matters most is our walk with God and we must take care of that before anything else. Even if the business is a failure its only temporal, to be unethical is to be immoral etc

Question Eight:If God is the standard for what is right and what is wrong (ethical or unethical) how can we effect change in our business or lives to show this?

- Always be an example, the way we live, work etc...is a witness to others
- Be honest and just, even when it doesn't work out in our favor
- When others ask you about things, don't be afraid to explain it and always stand for truth when pressured to compromise, others will be likely to follow your lead or atleast curtail their own activities when you're around.

Conclusion:

Ethics in general is concerned with human behavior that is acceptable or "right" and that which is not acceptable or "wrong" based on conventional morality. General ethical norms encompass truthfulness, honesty, integrity, respect for others, fairness, and justice. They relate to all aspects of life, including business and finance. It is all too easy to rationalize our way around many of these principles, but God will hold us accountable in the end. Ultimately, it is God whom we serve and to whom we must give account.

Synopsis:

True happiness comes from God. No other thing in this world can supply the joy we get from Jesus. In our world however millions of people will spend their lives in search of wealth and "toys" to fill the void in their lives when God is the true filler! Materialism is a spiritually lethal "ism" and must be avoided.

Ice-Breaker:

- **If you had an endless amount of money, what would you want to do?**
- **Will these things really make you happy?**

Introduction:

When I was a child, I really loved this snack (tell about a snack you loved). <Then, tell a story of how excited you got when you were able to have it. (i.e. how your grandmother had these at her house, and she'd always give them to you.)>
Perhaps, you had a favorite snack or a candy bar with similar story like mine. Does this snack make you as happy now as you were when you were five years old? I doubt it because now you can go to any store in town and buy one on your own. In some ways, it is now only a cheap, quick satisfaction. You see, what made you happy as a child is what makes you happy today. Often, we base our happiness on our perception of things. Consequently, what makes you happy changes as your life changes; your value systems adjust. Let's look further at this topic.

Question One: In the Declaration of Independence, writers penned this famous line: "...that they are endowed by their Creator with certain unalienable Rights, that among these are Life, Liberty and the pursuit of Happiness." It is commonly understood that the Founding Fathers meant the pursuit of properties and wealth. Does true happiness rest in the gaining of properties and wealth?

- Answers will vary.

Question Two: If we asked parents who have lost their children or children who have never had a loving family, blind men, those in abusive relationships or those who are lying on their death beds these questions, I wonder what their answers would be?

- More likely, our perspectives will change if some of these things we listed would seem like another candy bar.
- Wealth and possessions may satisfy you for a period but in the long run, they would not truly make you happy. Can we buy our happiness? Do things that we purchase really make us happy?

Question Three: Read Philippians 4:11-12. The theme of this passage is being content. What does it mean to be content?

- We must learn to be content with what God allows us to have rather than being hungry to attain for more than what we really need
- Always remember greed = love for money which is the root of all evil

Question Four: Let's study several things in **Philippians 4**. First let's read 4:4 and discuss what it means.

- Verse 4 clearly says to rejoice
- New Living Translation talks about being full of joy

Question Five: What is joy?

- Joy is a fruit of the Spirit according to Galatians 5
- True joy is experience when you are filled with the Spirit
- In the presence of God, there's a fullness of joy
- Joy of the Lord is my strength

Question Six: Let's read verse 7 and let's discuss what the verse is talking about.

- When you rejoice, God also gives us the peace of God
- Peace of God helps us to go beyond our understanding
- Peace of God helps us to learn to be content in situations that we may not fully comprehend or we have difficulty accepting

Question Seven: Let's read verses 13 and 19. The chance is you probably have read these verses and may even be able to quote. How do these verses connect to rest of Philippians 4 particularly 11-12

- We learn to be content because we know we can do all things through Christ which strengthens me
- We become content because we know that our God shall supply all of our need according to his riches in glory by Christ Jesus.
- These promises assure our faith and help us to be content.

Question Eight: So, can we list some keys that will help us to be content and experience true happiness?

- Answers will vary.

Conclusion:

In conclusion, we want you to know that God has everything that you need to make you happy. Just as these candies have made us happy for a moment when we were younger, material satisfaction can only make you happy for a period. Do not forget that God offers more than fleeting, material satisfactions.

While you may attain the wealth you need to obtain things those things that bring you satisfaction in life we hope that no matter what financial status you may be, you can find the true everlasting happiness in Christ through having Joy.

Synopsis:

Accidents happen to all of us and although we find it hard to see where God is, or why he allows us to go through such times, we must remember that God is on the throne and that no matter what happens to us, God is still in control and if we trust Him and serve Him faithfully, He will work all things out for our good!

Ice-Breaker:

- **How many of you have ever read the ending of a book before the beginning? Or skipped to the end to see how it all works out? How did that affect the overall story for you?**
- **Anyone remember those 3D art pictures where you have to take the whole picture in before the real image pops out at you? How long did it take before you saw the hidden image?**

Introduction:
Let's define an accident as a situation or incident in our life that has caused us pain, been traumatic, altered our lives unwillingly, resulted in disappointment or left us possibly bitter and angry. There are however, good accidents too. The Bible says in Matthew 5:45 that God sends the rain upon the just and the unjust. We know that God is in charge of everything, that His throne and Word are forever established and settled. God is in charge! So how can these things happen to us? How can these things possibly lead to anything good? Does God know what He's doing? Accidents are by definition unexpected generally and always leave us wondering about the unintended consequences. We all remember making mistakes as a child and falling back on the phrase "It was an accident." We didn't mean for it to happen, but did God? Let's explore the topic of the Divine Detour further.

Question One: If tomorrow morning everything you owned and everyone you loved were somehow gone or destroyed by some accident. How would you respond?

- Angry
- Sad
- Frustrated
- Disappointed

Question Two: Our situation above would be very similar to a rather famous story from the Bible. What do you know about Job? How did he respond?

- He was a Godly man
- Lost everything
- Ultimately restored
- Worshipped God, sought God

Question Three: How would it make you feel if you found out that life was just a random series of events and cosmic luck? If you believed the only truth in the universe was that "time and chance happens to all men?"

- Sad
- Pointless
- Indifferent
- Unsure

Question Four: Read **Ecclesiastes 3: 1-11**. What does the word "beautiful" mean to you?

- Unique
- Pretty/attractive
- Better than good/extraordinary
- Breathtaking/wonderful

Question Five: What's the difference between an accident and its consequences and our deliberate choices and their consequences?

- Willful vs. unwillful
- Our design vs. God's design
- Can show our weakness vs. can show our strength

Question Six: Read Psalm 139:15-16. What does our days being written out before they came to be remind you of or mean to you?

- An author about to write a book
- God knows our end from the beginning
- He knows what's going to happen to us

Question Seven: What's the purpose of a detour?

- To get you to your destination via a different or unplanned route
- A diversion to lead you away from something
- A safety mechanism to protect you from something dangerous ahead

Question Eight: Can you think of or name some accidents in your own life that have turned out to be beautiful?

- Students should share their own, if hesitant you may need to start things off etc…

Conclusion:

Accidents are not avoidable. It will happen. However, your response to accidents can show others about yourself and be an effective witness for Jesus. When things happen in our life and bring about the unintended consequences we must remember what He promised us in Hebrews 13:5 "God will never leave me nor forsake me." Even though we may not see what is happening or understand why God is allowing some things to happen to us, we must trust and know that God sees outside time and space, that He sees our ending from the very beginning. The Bible tell us that He is the author and finisher of our faith (Hebrews 12:2) and that He knows the plans that He has for us, plans to prosper us and give us an expected end (Jeremiah 29:11)! In Jobs situation, the enemy could do nothing to Job without first getting permission from God, which means God has a plan and purpose and a reason for everything that happens in your life and that what we see as troubles or trials or accidents, is really just a Divine Detour! Trust God to lead you, to form you and to finish the work He has

Be sure and check out:

<txHyphen.com>

For all the latest news and events for College and Career! You'll find event info, Bible Study material and so much more! Do yourself a favor and check it out!

txHyphen

a ministry for Young Adults

Also don't forget to visit:

texasyouth.net

For all the info and happenings of the Texas Youth! Don't miss an event, get the latest downloads and media, connect with others and reach this world!

www.ingramcontent.com/pod-product-compliance
Ingram Content Group UK Ltd.
Pitfield, Milton Keynes, MK11 3LW, UK
UKHW051133260726
13967UKWH00010B/3020